let's
stay
together

let's stay together

KARRY & CHERYL WESLEY

REDEMPTION
PRESS

Published by Redemption Press, PO Box 427, Enumclaw, WA 98022
Toll Free (844) 2REDEEM (273-3336)

Redemption Press is honored to present this title in partnership with
the author. The views expressed or implied in this work are those of
the author. Redemption Press provides our imprint seal representing
design excellence, creative content and high quality production.

All recited scriptures are from the *King James Version* unless
otherwise noted.

ISBN 13: 978-1-63232-437-5 (Print)
         978-1-63232-438-2 (ePub)
         978-1-63232-440-5 (Mobi)

Library of Congress Catalog Card Number: 2015940769

DEDICATION

We would like to dedicate this book to our children: Christopher (Sylan), Karl (Jasmine) and Charles. We hope and pray that we have served as good role models for you to see what a strong Christian marriage looks like. We would also like to dedicate this book to the married couples who are members of the Antioch Fellowship Church in Dallas. We hope that all of the sermons, seminars, and special sessions have helped to strengthen your marriages.

ACKNOWLEDGMENTS

Karry & Cheryl Wesley would like to thank the following for their contributions to *Let's Stay Together:*

Photography: Karl Wesley
Cover Design: Justin G. Bennett
Cover Photo Participants: Cornelius & Tavia Gibson

Previous Works by Karry Wesley

The Study of the Gospel of Mark

*If This Marriage Was Made in Heaven,
Why Am I Going Through Hell?*

*Hanging Tough in Tough Times
(Saints Staying Strong in Stormy Seasons)*

Rejoicing In The Lord (A Study of the Book of Philippians)

*Moving in the Wrong Direction
(The Study of the Book of Jonah)*

*Faith Without Works is Dead
(The Study of the Book of James)*

The Best is Yet to Come (The Study of the Book of Ruth)

To place an order of previous publications from
Dr. Wesley, please visit us at: www.afmbc.org

CONTENTS

LET'S STAY TOGETHER

Every institution established by God comes under attack by Satan. Since marriage is one of these institutions, Satan has increased his assault against it. Because of this, countless couples are choosing to end their marriages rather than taking a stand against the fiery darts of the enemy.

In this book, we hope to help married couples combat the attacks of the enemy by revealing strategies and weapons to use in the fight for their marriages. Also, it is our hope that singles will gain insight that will help them prepare for the divine institution of marriage, if it is the will of God for their lives.

We believe in the traditional and biblical view of marriage between a man and woman.

Chapter One

THE EASY OUT

The Culture Reflected

Although this book is not designed to take an in-depth look at the subject of divorce, we simply cannot ignore the matter. We acknowledge that married couples in the church are unfortunately getting divorced. We see this more every day.

First, we must deal with the *Alarming Stats* regarding divorce. A few years ago, when we starting conducting marriage conferences with several couples in attendance; we had the husbands and wives fill out questionnaires separately. One of the questions asked was if this was their first marriage. Each time we review the questionnaires from these conferences, it is alarming to discover that the majority in attendance have been married at least one other time. This is a frightening reality.

Next, we must address the *Attacked Saints* included in these statistics. Christians are not excluded. Most of our churches are filled with people who have been divorced, so it's not just happening to those "in the world." Sadly, divorce occurs among believers and non-believers alike.

What is even more alarming is the fact that divorce has become an *Acceptable Step* for couples with problems to take. It is no longer considered the last option for couples; instead, divorce has become so common that many people prepare (at least mentally) for a divorce while planning their marriages.

From a spiritual perspective, the *Acknowledged Source* of the growing numbers of divorced people is Satan. He has increased his assault against the institution of marriage. Since God established the institution of marriage and hates divorce, He will never lead us to the divorce court. On the other hand, Satan will do everything in his power to cause married couples to become so miserable with each other that they find it easier to divorce rather than commit to working on the marriage.

As believers, we must start acting like the *Armed Saints* we have been called to be. As Christians, we have been empowered to combat the attacks of the enemy. Spirit-filled believers are equipped to prevent the weapons formed against us by the enemy from prospering. This includes the warfare against our marriages.

The Common Reasons

Let's examine some of the leading causes of divorce in our nation and churches today.

The most common cause is *Adultery*. In the context of this book, adultery deals with a spouse having an intimate physical relationship outside of the marriage. Adultery simply means that a spouse chose to engage in sexual intercourse with someone other than his/her spouse. No matter what society condones, adultery is still unacceptable to God.

Then there are the *Affairs* that seep in and destroy marriages. It is true that an affair can ultimately lead to adultery but we are speaking of the stage before it reaches that point. Unlike adultery, affairs may have a strong emotional attachment, rather than a sexual one. These relationships usually begin innocently enough, like having lunch with a co-worker of the opposite sex. The conversations gradually move from business-related concerns to personal matters, and before you know it, the relationship grows more intimate.

The societal ill called spousal *Abuse* has increased over the years. One spouse abuses or mistreats the other in a variety of ways: physically, emotionally, and/or financially. None is acceptable. God never intended for a spouse to be abused. When physical abuse occurs in a marriage, we always encourage the abused victim to leave the spouse immediately for safety reasons.

If the victim is not ready to leave, she is given valuable resources and encouraged to seek ongoing professional counseling. Through this process, it is hoped that a plan of escape is developed. It is our belief that the abuser must be reformed before there is to be any consideration of restoration. The victim should not return home unless there is an undeniable proof of the change.

Another cause of divorce is *Addiction*. The mate(s) has addictions to drugs, drinking, pornography, gambling, excessive spending, etc. that cause problems for the couple. When you have one or both individuals in the marriage addicted to something that is not healthy, it will have a negative impact on the individual and the relationship.

Another common reason for divorce is *Abandonment*. One of the spouses has decided to leave and stay away. This is not just related to relocating physically. The spouse may have decided to relocate emotionally (no affection), spiritually (missing ethics or morals), financially (refuses to pay bills), etc. When there is abandonment by one or both parties, it usually leads to divorce.

Several common reasons for divorce have been listed thus far. However, we believe the most common reason is connected to the *Attitudes* of married couples. Without a biblical foundation, the wrong attitude will exist. Many people enter marriage without a true biblical foundation or understanding of this divine institution established by the Lord.

We must stop thinking of marriage as a consumer relationship. If we don't alter our mind-sets, we will always want a refund or an exchange because there is no perfect product. When marriage is treated as a consumer relationship, you're constantly looking for ways to get out of it. If there is someone you see whom you like better, you end the present relationship. If you don't agree with what he or she says, you exchange your spouse for someone else. From the beginning in the Garden with Adam and Eve, it was not so.

In Mark 10, the Pharisees came to Jesus to ask a question about divorce. "Is it lawful for a man to put away his wife?" Matthew adds, "for every cause" (Matthew 19:3). The background of this question includes the morally loose societal influence of Jesus' day – even in the Jewish society. Marriage was considered no more than a business transaction, a piece of paper.

If it worked, fine; if it didn't work, divorce. One could always divorce (see Matthew 5:31). They asked about divorce but Jesus gave them an answer about marriage (see Mark 10:5-9). Why would Jesus give a response related to marriage instead of divorce? It was primarily due to the fact that the institution of marriage had been de-emphasized while divorce was prioritized in that society. That mind-set really hasn't changed much.

The Cohesion Removed

There is *The Biblical Mandate*. Cohesion is the action of sticking together. It is God's desire for the husband and wife to cleave to each other and become one. The Word of God says, "For this cause shall a man [or woman] leave his father and mother and cleave to his wife [or husband]. What therefore God hath joined together, let not man put asunder" (See Mark 10:7-9).

Instead of seeing couples cleaving, we are spending a lot of time addressing *The Broken Marriages* that exist in our society and sanctuaries. By the way, the marriage can be broken while you are still legally married and living together. There are many who believe the cohesion is removed only when a divorce has occurred. We disagree. Husbands and wives can be living in the same house but separated. It is possible for your marriage to be broken while you are sleeping in the same bed and riding in the same car. The phase, "Let not man put asunder," is not just a reference to the divorce lawyer. It also applies to us individually.

Let's address *The Blamed Mate* responsible for removing the cohesion. According to one spouse, the other spouse is always the problem in the marriage. We hear it all the time. "If our husbands would love us as Christ loved the church," marriages would not be in trouble. If our wives would "submit to their own husbands" as the Bible commands, marriages would not be in trouble. It is easy to play the blame game. However, we contend that there is enough blame to go around.

In this book, we are going to focus on *The Blessed Miracle* that God desires to perform in our marriages to cause couples to cleave together "until death they do part." If couples are willing, God is able!

Chapter Two

HOME IMPROVEMENT NEEDED

Some years ago, I applied for a "home improvement loan." On the application, I had to include information about the "need for the loan." It was needed for three reasons. First, it was needed for the purpose of repairing some items in the house. Secondly, it was needed for some remodeling, and finally, it was needed to replace some things. After receiving the loan and taking care of repairing, remodeling; and replacing items, restoration had taken place. The house almost looked brand new.

Marriage enrichment can be compared to a home improvement loan. From a spiritual perspective, we need a face lift. This does not mean that everything is in bad shape, but an area or two might need improvement.

We needed the home improvement loan *To Repair* some items in the house. Repairs (major and minor) are often needed in our relationships to deal with things that are broken. There were broken items in our house that we did not discard because we knew those items could be saved. In some cases, it required minor work. In others, it required long hours to repair.

We had a washer that did not complete the spin cycle, so when clothes were pulled from it, they were still soaked. For months, we pulled out soaking clothes and squeezed the excess water from them. When the technician came to repair the washer, I was amazed to see that it took less than five minutes to correct the problem, and it only took one turn of a screw.

In marriage, the same principle is true. Repairs are possible, and in some cases, very little work is required. You simply need to know which screw to turn.

Next, we needed the home improvement loan *To Remodel*. We wanted a new look in some of the rooms. This was not the goal for the whole house (just certain rooms). The walls needed repainting because of the wear and tear that came from three active boys growing up there.

In some marriages, the relationship is okay but a new look is needed. The cycles of life have resulted in a lot of wear and tear. You end up getting in a rut and never attempting to change the environment. But you can remodel that area in your marriage, if you'd like.

We also needed the home improvement loan *To Replace* some items. No, we are not talking about replacing your spouse here but about the need to replace some of the views and philosophies related to marriage that are not biblically sound.

Several items in our house needed to be replaced. Those items were not working at all. They were still in the original position (dishwasher, microwave, etc.) but repairing them was too costly. All of the items worked great when we first purchased them. After years of usage by us and our three sons that came later, the appliances eventually stopped working. It was better to replace those items with new ones. In our marriages, we must look at getting rid of the old ways that are not working and replacing them with workable ways. Before the children came along, date nights happened weekly. After boys were born and parental involvement took over, the date nights stopped happening. We had to come up with a creative plan to replace this wonderful experience by shifting it from date night to date day.

Lastly, we needed the home improvement loan *To Restore* some items in the house. We had a few items that were in pretty good shape but restoration was needed to bring out the glitter that had once existed. Some tables needed to have the old varnish removed and a new coat applied. The tables were salvageable but restoration was required. Restoration is needed in our marriages, too. The marriage is still working but some polishing and upholstering will enhance it.

The Conflict Rising

In every marriage, there's going to be conflict. Experts have said there are four broad categories of conflict in marriage: money, sex, communication, and children. But in reality, some have even ended their marriages over much smaller things like *squeezing the toothpaste tube the wrong way, leaving towels on the bathroom floor, putting empty milk containers back in the refrigerator, leaving newspapers in sections all over the sofa, leaving the toilet seat up, or replacing the tissue.* It's hard to believe, but it's true.

How do we keep wedlock from turning into deadlock? We need a clear understanding of the reasons for conflict in marriage. Let's take a closer look at some of them.

We must start with *The Devil's Plan.* You will face the constant attacks of the enemy in your marriage. If God is for it, Satan is opposed to it. The devil does not desire for your marriage to thrive or survive. It is not that he is out to get you, but he is opposed to anything that God is for. Remember that all institutions established by

God are under constant attack or assault by the enemy. The family, including marriage, is on the list.

When Jesus established the church, He informed us that the gates of hell will not prevail against it. He didn't say the gates of hell would not *try* to prevail. Satan works really hard to plant the thought of divorce when conflict surfaces. You need to be aware of this goal of Satan. By the way, the devil doesn't mind if you stay married, as long as there is a constant battle going on.

Let's take a look at *The Different Perspectives* couples bring into the marriage. Conflict comes when two very different people, with varied experiences and mind-sets, live in the same space twenty-four hours a day. No two people are alike. Their individual approaches to situations often bring challenges to their marriage.

For many couples, rather than being complementary, their differences cause conflict. Think about it—two very different lives become one. Since perspectives are developed over several years, it takes time to change. And that's not always easy.

The different perspectives are usually the result of *The Diverse Pasts* of the marriage partners. A lot of what we do as adults stems from what we saw happen when we were children. We often exhibit behaviors from our families of origin and our backgrounds. This does not mean, however, that you will become an alcoholic because you grew up in a home with alcoholics (or abuse, drug addiction, etc.). Although we are shaped by our environment, behavior is learned. The good news is that negative behaviors can be unlearned.

Next, let's talk about *The Designed Personalities* in your marriage. You were wonderfully and uniquely made by God, and so was your spouse. While it is true that opposites attract, it is also true that you must learn to live with the opposite personality that you have been attracted to. It is absolutely necessary that you learn to adjust to your spouse. It can be challenging, but you don't want to be married to someone "just like you." If you think there is conflict now, it would be far worse if your spouse were exactly like you.

We have *The Defective Partners* in the marriage. We are all imperfect and we bring those imperfections into the relationship. You didn't become perfect when you exchanged vows with your spouse. You carried your imperfections over into the marriage. We must commit to continuously work on personal imperfections and issues in order to reduce conflict.

We need to mention *The Dangerous Practice* that has led to a lot of conflict in marriage. We permit too many people in our business. A lot of conflict comes into the marital relationship because we listen to a lot of outside sources. We let coworkers, family members, talk show hosts and others plant thoughts in our minds that lead to conflict. Last, there is *The Destructive Principle* we must constantly guard against. We are naturally inclined to look out for number one. The most damaging cause of conflict in marriage is the fact that we are self-centered. When life is about having everything "my way," it doesn't matter what the other desires. When you have lived independently most of your life, you often take that mind-set into the marriage.

The Counseling Requests

Before continuing, let's make one point clear. Many Christian couples reading this book or attending a marriage seminar or retreat will not resolve the major conflicts that may exist in their marriages in one attempt. Some issues are just too complex to resolve in these types of venues, within such a small window of time.

As a pastor, I am often approached with requests for marriage counseling. I usually respond by saying, "I will talk or consult with you, but I stopped trying to provide counseling services years ago." This comment usually leads to shock until I explain it further. True counseling is a full-time job. I believe most pastors will agree with me for the reasons below.

First, *The Lengthy Sessions* are needed to really resolve marital conflict. Counseling requires many hours of meeting. In order to effectively counsel people, the counselor must meet several times with couples and others to reach a breakthrough point. It is extremely difficult to resolve issues with a meeting or two.

Next, I believe *The Loaded Schedule* of the average pastor prevents effectiveness in counseling with couples dealing with a lot of marital conflict. Most pastors have too much on their plates to effectively lead couples down the path of reconciliation and restoration. It is extremely difficult to make scheduling adjustments to meet with couples when a pastor's schedule is already packed. When you consider the number of people desiring counseling, it would be impossible to schedule those meetings as well as perform the other responsibilities associated with overseeing a congregation.

Many couples believe if they sit down with the pastor, he can tell them what to do to remedy the problem, when it is not that simple. A lot of marriage conflict stems from *The Locked-up Stuff* in the lives of the couple. Issues and problems that are not immediately apparent or easy to identify, have been carried with them for years.

The objective of counseling is to get to the root of the problem. But in most cases, you are not dealing with the obvious. As a matter of fact, many issues presently being dealt with in our lives can be traced all the way back to encounters we had with others between childhood and now.

The main reason for making these claims is connected to *The Limited Skills* of the average pastor. The average pastor possesses limited counseling skills when it comes to dealing with deep-seated psychological issues. There are exceptions, but a degree in theology does qualify a pastor to provide ongoing counseling.

Some congregations are blessed with *The Licensed Source* to address needs for counseling services for marital issues and other psychological matters.

If counseling requests can't be fulfilled at our churches, what can the church do to help married couples? As pastors, we must make sure *The Learning Stations* are in place to help couples with their marriages. Learning stations refer to sermons, classes, and seminars that help people with their marriages. The church can make sure that programs exist to minister to the needs of the people and help marriages survive and thrive.

Chapter Three

THE SPIRITUAL INSTITUTION

The Cover Reviewed

Take a look at the cover of this book for a moment. What message do you get from this picture?

As we examine the picture, we noticed that the *Bible* immediately stands out. The main manual for marriage is God's Word. The Bible must serve as the primary manual used to maintain healthy relationships. We must continuously apply the Word of God to our marriages in order for the spiritual glue to remain.

The *Bodies* on the cover are physically close together. Regardless of the challenges the couple could be enduring, they have positioned themselves in a way that makes it difficult for anything (or anyone) to come between them.

The *Brokenness* is visible as you look at the faces of the couple. The tears could indicate pain and brokenness that have been experienced in the relationship. Since love is based on a heart connection, married couples sometimes experience heartache in their relationships.

Next, you have the *Bond*. The interlocked hands represent the bond between the couple. It's as if they are saying, "I am going to hold on to you no matter what. I may have been wounded emotionally but the grip remains."

Although the couple has been wounded, you see them *Bowing*. The couple is in a powerful position of prayer. Prayer still changes things and is the believer's greatest weapon. When married couples learn how to keep their marriages saturated with prayer, blessings will come.

Did you notice the cross in the *Background*? It reminds us of redemption and reconciliation. It reminds us of faith and forgiveness. It reminds us that God commended His love toward us while we were yet sinners and died for us.

There is another point about the Bible in the picture. It serves as the *Blocker*. The Bible is blocking their view of each other. In the epistle of James, the Bible is described as a glass or mirror. It reveals our true image. It shows us that there are areas in our lives in need of work. When we keep our eyes on the Word and obey it, our marriages will thrive.

The Conversion Required

How can there be so many believers ending their marriages when they know God hates divorce? How can there be so many Christian spouses fussing and fighting? Why are believers involved in extramarital affairs? Could it be due to the fact that neither or only one member in the relationship is saved from the penalty we deserve as sinners because Jesus died for those sins on the cross? You cannot have a marriage operating according to the divine plan without the wife and husband both being saved.

Marriage must be viewed as *The Divine Institution* if it is to work as God intended. Marriage is an institution established by God. Since He established the institution, it cannot flow as God intended if married persons are not connected to Him properly.

You are married to a person who falls into one of the following categories: the natural State (has no relationship with Jesus), the carnal State (has a relationship with Jesus as Savior but not as Lord) or the spiritual State (Jesus Christ is Savior and Lord). The institution works best when spiritual men and spiritual women are united in holy matrimony. However, this is not always what takes place. If you are spiritual and your spouse is natural/carnal, you are unequally yoked.

For someone reading this book, *The Divorce Initiative* probably crossed your mind when we discussed being unequally yoked. However, if one of the spouses is not converted, this does not justify ending the marriage. You don't have divine permission to bail out if your spouse is not saved. According to the Word of God (which is the tool that spiritual people abide by), you cannot do this (1 Corinthians 7:12-16; 1 Peter 3:1).

If your spouse is not saved, your prayers should be linked to *The Desired Identification* with Jesus Christ. Your ultimate desire should be to see your spouse identify with the same Lord you have accepted in your life. As a Christian, our primary mission is to lead people to Christ (even if it is my spouse). The Bible speaks of your spouse being won by your conversation, that is, our Christian lifestyle. If your spouse does not have a relationship with the Lord, it is important to focus on the soul of your "soul-mate."

Let us make one more point here. You should view your unsaved spouse as *The Deliverable Individual*. If God saved you and me, He can save anybody. Your spouse is not beyond the reach of God.

The Christian Repenting

It is important to repent of past sins. Repentance involves more than seeking forgiveness for the sin committed. It also involves turning away from that sin, so that you are not trapped by it in the future.

Your marriage will not get better without addressing the *Sins Committed*. Every married person reading this book has sinned within the marriage. You have said something, thought something, or done something sinful. None of us is exempt from this indictment. We are all guilty.

Do you feel bad about the sins you have committed? If so, deal with the *Sorrow Connected* with those sins. By the way, godly sorrow accompanies true repentance. When we really repent, it flows from the heart and not the head (see 2 Corinthians 7:8-10).

Next, a *Serious Commitment* to live better arises. Repentance without renewal is not good. When we repent, we not only seek forgiveness of our sins. We also seek heavenly assistance to help us avoid that road in the future(see 1 John 1:9).

The Confirmation Received

We struggle with people saying they have received divine confirmations from God to end their marriages when it goes against biblical principles.

In most cases, the initial decision to pursue divorce proceedings surfaces as a result of *The Scattered Emotions* connected to some hurtful action on the part of the spouse. We often make decisions based on how we feel in the moment. Since we have been wounded and hurt, we start looking at the emotional roller coaster as confirmation from God to exit the marriage.

In all honesty, *The Scriptural Endorsement* is not the starting point when making life-altering decisions like divorce. As believers, we should always try to line up with His Word. I always question people who tell me they prayed about something and the Lord confirmed it when it goes against the Word.

When we strive to save our marriages, *The Satanic Encounter* proves and confirms that we are doing something right. It is important to remember that Satan opposes anything established by God. If you're not careful, he will send signals to confuse you, causing you to easily fall for his lies.

The Considered Roots

Conflict and confrontation are the fruit of our problems. We must try to get to the root of the problem in order to resolve it.

Let's deal with the *Fairy Tale* aspects of our beliefs. People enter marriage with a false view or perspective.

Many want the fairy tale wedding, and having a great deal of money can make this a reality.

It is impossible, however, to have a fairy tale marriage. You cannot live "happily ever after." The reason is the *Flawed Tenants* in the house. Two flawed people exchanged vows at your wedding. The reasons there are problems in the house can be linked to the imperfect people residing there.

The *Forsaken Truth* created this mess and misery. Forsaking God's truth always leads to problems. Most marital issues come into existence as a result of us failing to do things according to the Word of God. Consequences come when we ignore the Word of God.

The Frequent Temptations come to test our commitment. The moment we became Christians, the Holy Spirit moved into our lives. Although He moved in, the lust of the flesh did not move out. The flesh did not depart the day you became saved, nor when you exchanged wedding vows. We must crucify the flesh daily in order to walk in victory in all arenas of life.

Yes, your troubles are legitimate but you must always approach each issue with the faith that it is *Fixable Trouble*. God can help us resolve all issues. Although there is no such thing as a "problem-free marriage," your connection with Christ means that you know the "problem-solver."

Most couples believe they need a major overhaul in order to save their marriages. However, we believe that in most cases, a minor tune-up will get the marriage on track.

Chapter Four

THE RIGHT CHOICE

The Choice Regretted

At times, we look at our marriages and wish we had said, "I don't" rather than "I do." We discovered so many things after the vows. Not only did we discover things about our spouse, but also about ourselves. You may have discovered how selfish you are, or even worse, how "quick-tempered" you are.

In retrospect, the *Dating Phase* has often become a faded memory for couples. The romance in its infancy was unexplainable, unbelievable, and incredible. During the dating season, he was like a dream and she was a breath of fresh air. You counted the moments until you would talk again and longed for your next date. You could hardly wait.

Then there was the *Dazzling Proposal* that swept both of you off your feet. It was a memorable event. One day, you practiced how you would propose and you went over it again and again in your mind. The proposal was so dazzling that it brought joy to your heart and tears to your eyes at the same time.

The *Dedication Period* began on that day when you exchanged vows. You were standing next to the person that you planned to spend the rest of your life with. You were on cloud nine as you looked into each other's eyes and promised to dedicate your life "until death do us part."

As the *Days Passed*, you tried to keep the activity of your courtship alive in the marriage. You attempted various things to make your spouse happy. You rushed home to your wife. You couldn't wait to see your husband. It was almost a replica of your courtship.

The *Daily Presence* of your spouse led to the unexpected being revealed. After settling in the marriage, something happened. As time passed, you learned that it was not a replica of your days of courtship, as you had desired. You are now with your spouse more than anyone else, which makes it difficult to manufacture those moments of surprise and wonder.

After being married for a while, you go through the *Discovery Process*, which is a learning experience. As a result of being around your spouse all the time, you have learned some things that you didn't know. While you were dating, only the "best foot" forward was presented. You have noticed some dark spots that you didn't see before. It could be due to the fact that you were so "in love" that you didn't notice. Maybe this is what people mean when they say, "Love is blind."

Initially, you were madly in love with your spouse. Now, you are the *Disappointed Partner* due to the new revelations. Some of the discoveries have caused you to question the move you made to marry. It has reached the point that you have forgotten about the good days, and you're now questioning why you married in the first place. You have become so disappointed with your partner that your love is no longer blind. The problem, however, is that you're only seeing what's wrong.

Now there is the *Divorce Pondered.* In some cases, you have given thoughtful consideration to divorcing your spouse, even if you haven't brought it to your spouse's attention. You have decided that this is not the man or woman you thought you married and you are ready to end it. You want your dream realized.

The marriage is really in trouble when you reach the point of making *Departure Plans.* When you reach the point of mapping out a plan or strategy to leave, Satan will help you out. He doesn't want you to work on ways to restore what you once had with your spouse.

The Calculated Risks

When the departure from the marriage is based on attitudes rather than abandonment, adultery, addictions, or abuse, we think we will be better off. We think the grass is greener on the other side. It is a calculated risk that requires deeper thought.

We acknowledge that the *Honeymoon Stage* has ended for some reading this material. For some, the honeymoon phase ended abruptly. In other cases, it is hard to pinpoint exactly when it ended and what actually took place. In most cases, it was a combination of things that caused the marriage to get off track.

Heated Sessions with your spouse have become commonplace, and you're tired of them. After the last occurrence, you decided that you couldn't take anymore. You are tired of the heartache, and as a result of the miserable moments, you have concluded that things will be better without your spouse.

Since you are now fed up, you take the *Hasty Step* to end your marriage. You make the decision to get out and find yourself saying, "I can do better by myself." Or even worse, you believe that someone else will make you happier.

The marriage is over, and for the moment you convince yourself that you are enjoying this *Happy Season* without your spouse. You decided to exit the marriage and for a season, it appears to be better. Finally, you no longer have to put up with his/her ways. In some cases, a spouse immediately connects with another person and is happy as a lark again.

Yes, you are happy for a season but suddenly *Hell Surfaces* in this new relationship. You begin to repeat the steps discussed in the "choice regretted" again, forgetting that Satan will never show you the whole picture when he tempts you to go against the perfect will of God. Statistics show there is a higher rate of divorce among second and third marriages. You mistakenly thought that the "grass was greener on the other side" and that your life would be better. But you were wrong.

The Challenging Rescue

Why is it so difficult to help couples deal with their marital issues?

First, it deals with the *Undesired Action.* Some couples don't want to put forth the effort to fix what is broken. They don't want to take the actions necessary to improve their marriages. We have learned that you can offer seminars and sessions designed to salvage marriages on the brink of disaster, but some couples have no desire whatsoever to be rescued. Many have been wounded so deeply that they would prefer for the marriage to just end.

Then there are the *Unwilling Admissions*. It is challenging to salvage a marriage when only one person is willing to admit that mistakes were made and change is required. The spouse who insists that the marriage failure is solely due to the other person hinders any attempt to resolve matters.

Another difficulty is the *Unforgiving Attitude* that exists with some. A spouse's refusal to forgive makes it hard to repair the marriage. When there is not a commitment to forgive the spouse for a past mistake, it is hard to rescue the couple.

We often deal with couples with *Unmanageable Anger* issues. There are wives afraid to talk to their husbands and husbands afraid to talk to their wives due to anger management concerns. The spouse will explode if the problem is mentioned. The couple cannot have a normal conversation without explosive anger manifesting itself. They walk around on pins and needles because the explosion can happen at any moment.

The one that shocks us the most is *Unsanctioned Affairs*. Remaining connected to an outside relationship can prevent healing. In some cases, married couples have become emotionally and possibly physically attached to someone outside of the marriage and they refuse to end these relationships. It is sad that they don't see the damage caused by them and they are unwilling to end them. It is even worse when they try to justify a relationship's continuation.

It is extremely challenging to rescue couples who continue to listen to *Ungodly Advisors* who have absolutely nothing to do with the Word of God. It is hard to help married couples when they are willing to listen to the advice of ungodly people rather than righteous people who use the Word of God to offer advice.

The Claimed Restoration

If you really want to fight for your marriage, you need some help from the One who established the institution. We claim that there is power in the Name of Jesus to do anything; therefore, we should be bold enough to claim restoration for our marriages.

A *Christian Focus* is required for restoration to take place. What is the Christian thing to do? As believers, we have the responsibility to demonstrate Christ-like behavior in all relationships. The marital relationship is included.

Charismatic Flavor is applicable in our marriages. The Christian with charismatic flavor believes God will give us the desires of heart if we only believe. Therefore, we pray in faith believing He will restore broken relationships. We boldly name and claim the results in Jesus' name. I am amazed that we become charismatic about everything but the right things. We are quick to "name it and claim it" when we cannot support it scripturally. For instance, you shouldn't name and claim that a new house is going to be received when you cannot afford the mortgage.

With our marriages, however, this is not the case. We can "name restoration and claim it" because we can do something about it. We need to declare our belief that God can save our marriage. Additionally, we need to take a stand and refuse to allow the devil to get the victory.

Restoration cannot happen without the *Consolidated Faith* of the couple. As faith partners, we must believe in His power to save the marriage. It works best when both the husband and wife believe God for the same thing. When your faith is combined with your spouse's, mountains will move.

Faith in God is only a part of the process. The *Collaborative Fix* is required to bring about restoration. It must be a combined effort of God and us. God can fix every area of the marriage if we are willing to do our part. It is true that God has the power to fix the marriage, but we must be willing to follow His instructions. God expects it to be a coordinated and collaborative effort from those involved. It will not be a quick fix. It took time for you to get to the place where you are and it will take some time to fix what has been messed up.

Last, restored Christian marriages are linked to the *Chosen Favor*. The favor of God is available by choice and not by force. It is true that God desires to show favor to those who belong to Him, but it is our choice. He will never force His way on us. Yes, He can fix troubled marriages but the couple must accept what God offers.

Chapter Five

LET'S TALK ABOUT IT

The Cutting Rhetoric

Have you said these words? "He knows what to say to tick me off" or "She knows what to say to get under my skin"? There are times when we say things designed to create pain as a way of retaliation. Yes, it even happens in marriage.

We must continuously work on how we talk to each other. We must beware of the *Chosen Vulgarity* that can come from our mouths. We choose to live holy or not to live holy. Listen to these statements. "She made me so angry that I had to curse her out." "He made me curse because he kept pushing my buttons." Make no mistake: using profanity is a choice. No one can force you to "curse like a sailor," even when you are angry.

Let's say that you never use profanity when talking to your spouse. That's great, but using a *Crushing Voice* can be just as problematic. The way you speak and the tone of your voice can also cut and crush your spouse. You don't have to curse a person to hurt him or her. The volume of your voice and the words you emphasize can cause just as much damage.

As a result of the stress-filled society we live in, we often see the *Camouflaged Venting* creeping into our marriages. There are times when cutting rhetoric comes as a result of being unable to vent or express ourselves in other areas. You may have wanted to give your employer a "piece of your mind" all day because of what he did to you (low performance rating, demotion, being overlooked for promotion, etc.). You wisely chose not to act on your thoughts due to the consequences your actions would bring.

Instead, however, you heaped that anger and frustration onto your wife, who did not have dinner ready on time. The real issue wasn't about dinner being late or about your wife, for that matter. You had to let off steam and you did it the wrong way.

The Communication Required

Your marriage will never be strong if good and healthy communication does not exist. The base or foundation of a successful marriage is effective communication. When married couples learn how to communicate like Christian adults, most issues can be resolved. Communication is the fundamental foundation of every successful marriage. Without it, the couple will be miserable. By the way, just because you talk a lot does not mean you are properly communicating. In the next chapter, we will discuss the steps involved in proper communication.

A misconception of many couples is that the length of time we've been with our spouse should minimize the need for communication. We think because we have been with a person for a long time, our spouse should know when things are wrong without our verbalizing it. We call this one the *Closed Bridge*. The bridge of communication must reopen if you as a couple are to pass over the issues.

Imagine that you are driving to your destination when the drawbridge ahead of you goes up unexpectedly. You cannot get to the other side until that bridge comes down or reopens. When the bridge of communication is closed, it is hard to crossover to understanding or get past the issues you face in your marriage. If the line of communication is not open, you cannot resolve the issues that surface in marriage until you are once again able to communicate effectively.

Next, let's deal with the *Conflict Blamed* for the closed bridge. As mentioned before, conflict is not the root but the fruit of the problem we're having in our marriage. We often blame past conflict for the lack of communication in the marriage. Communicating with each other can resolve the conflict. The failure to talk and listen (the root) often leads to the conflict and emotional pain (the fruit). Proper communication will often prevent the conflict from escalating. As a result of communication problems, you end up with unresolved conflict.

The *Constant Badgering* can prevent open, effective communication from taking place. If the same issues resurface over and over, proper communication is probably missing. One sign of a lack of communication in marriage can be seen when you continue to badger your spouse about the unresolved conflict.

Couples will never be able to communicate properly without addressing the *Common Blockers* that keep us from properly tuning in and focusing on each other. Effective communication requires the couple's undivided attention. Busy schedules, children, fear, television, telephones, and dozens of other distractions can block couples from communicating properly. Although these are inevitable, they can all be managed so that successful communication can take place.

Chapter Six

THE DIVINE FIX

The Conversations Restored

It is easy for couples to get into a rut of holding onto their concerns, fears, and even dreams instead of sharing them with each other. When this is done over time, it becomes a wedge that can cause spouses to grow apart. When that happens, it is time for couples to take special steps to restore what has been lost.

Whenever we address communication, we must start off with the reality of the *Daily Tasks* that we all have in our lives. Daily schedules are filled with required activities from work to children's events and volunteer obligations. We have so much going on, that it becomes extremely difficult to complete our tasks by the end of the day. With all that's being done by couples, effectively communicating with each other has been omitted. More than anything else, good communication has to be an intentional addition to our schedules.

We must start with the *Designated Time* to communicate. Finding time to communicate with your spouse must be prioritized above other things. You need to have some "uninterrupted couple time" to converse about life. We encourage you to start off with a commitment of at least one hour each day of uninterrupted communication time.

If communication has disappeared in your marriage, you may need to come up with the *Determined Topics* in advance. Without a plan for topics, you could end up all over the place. At times, the conversation must be specific rather than general. On one hand, you don't want to limit the topics and on the other hand, you don't want to ignore key concerns that you need to discuss. There are two important questions to ask on a regular basis:

1. "How are you doing?"
2. "How are we doing?"

We recommend that you designate key areas where you will communicate with your spouse. Let's call this the *Discussion Table*. Although identified as a table, it can be any area conducive to relaxing conversation. It can be the kitchen table or the car as you are driving to work. One place we strongly discourage is the bedroom, unless it is absolutely necessary.

In your time of discussion, it's imperative that one person not dominate. It works best when *Different Turns* are taken. Remember that this is the time of sharing for both the husband and wife. It is a time for talking and for listening. You should always know how to push the "pause button" to allow your spouse to speak.

During this exercise, keep the *Divine Temperament* of your spouse in mind. One of you may not be naturally talkative. When a person doesn't talk a lot because he or she was divinely designed this way, the other should not force the spouse to change. Rather, accept his or her one or two comments as full participation. On the other hand, the one who talks excessively should remain aware of his or her spouse's attention to the conversation. A lengthy dialogue is no guarantee that your spouse is still listening. The talkative one should also pause periodically to allow the other to add his or her brief comments.

Before moving from this exercise, we must comment on the *Devil's Tactic* again. Expect the devil to try to invade the premises during this time of communication. The devil will always try his best to turn this time into a "fussing frenzy." He knows that effective conversations can prevent current and future turmoil.

Before wrapping up the exercise, delineate the *Decided Tasks*. We often come up with a list of action plans in our minds but never communicate them with our spouses. Conclude the session by repeating the action items you both have agreed to perform. This allows you to leave the discussion table in one accord.

The Comments Rehearsed

As mentioned before, we have all made mistakes in our marriages. None of us is perfect, including our spouses. Since we fall short of perfection and "blow it" periodically, there are several comments we should rehearse over and over again.

The first is the *Admitted Mistake* that will take place in marriage. It is the simplest yet most difficult thing for most of us to do. When we blow it, mess up, or commit a wrong, we need to admit it to our spouses. As Christian adults, it is imperative that we own up to our mess-ups. You will never enjoy marital bliss if you refuse to admit your mistakes when they happen. In doing this, make sure you are specific in describing the incorrect choice you made.

Admitting your mistakes is great but your *Apology Matters* most. Acknowledging wrong is not the final step. An acknowledgment of wrong without an apology is not beneficial. After acknowledging the mistake, an apology should immediately follow.

The *Attached Message* to complete the process involves including specifically what you are apologizing for. It is good to apologize for your act and to acknowledge your desire not to do it again. For example, "I did wrong when I lied about taking the money out of the account and I want to do right in the future."

The *Appealed Mercy* is next. The Bible teaches us to be merciful like our heavenly Father. We need mercy from the one who was offended. Mercy defined is "not getting what one rightly deserves." Therefore, when we seek forgiveness from our spouses, we are asking for mercy. It is important to ask, "Will you forgive me for what I did?"

A few more things need to be considered before we move on. The *Appropriate Moment* of your apology is important, and it matters. When you have offended your spouse and caused wounds to occur, negative emotions are running rampant. You may have to give your spouse a few moments to calm down before apologizing. Make sure, however, that you do not allow too much time to elapse before implementing the steps.

There is also the matter of the *Allowed Mulling* by the one offended. You may receive an immediate acceptance of the apology; however in some cases, the one offended may need to contemplate the apology before accepting it. If your spouse has been deeply wounded by your actions, it may take some time to get over it.

Don't be guilty of the *Aborted Mission* that can easily surface. An inappropriate apology can make matters worse. The objective is to sincerely apologize for the personal mistake you made. It is meaningful when it is done because we regret what we have done. The apology loses power when comments are made like: "I was wrong when I said what I said. I am sorry that I cursed at you *but* you shouldn't have done what you did." The minute you add the conjunction *but,* you have aborted your mission.

Chapter Seven

EFFECTIVE PROBLEM-SOLVING TOOLS

The Conflict Resolved

In this chapter, we want to outline several practical steps to resolve conflict. In doing so, we are using acronyms so that you will hopefully memorize each one and reflect on them often.

STEP (Spend Time Effectively Praying): Pray before you say anything. In Proverbs 16:1, the writer says, "The preparation of the heart in man, and the answer of the tongue, is from the Lord." Sometimes it is hard to say what needs to be said. James says, "The effectual fervent prayer of a righteous man availeth much" (James 5:16b). The best way to assure that you say the right thing is to spend time in prayer first.

PATCH (Pray About The Current Hostility): If you are bitter, tell God about it. The first part of Proverbs 16:1 focuses on the "preparations of the heart in man." Conflict creates pain and heartache. It cannot be resolved when the pain is the primary focus. When people focus on the pain caused by others, they usually become hostile. Therefore, the starting point is to get a grip on the hostility. How can you do this? You must seek assistance from your Lord and Savior. Without Him, it is impossible to patch up the conflict.

FAST (Forget About Selfish Treasures): Always focus on "us" rather than "me." Conflict can never be resolved when it is all about "what you want or have" without considering your spouse. You cannot be prideful or selfish if you desire to resolve conflict. The resolution should not be about you but "us."

TEAM (The Egos Are Missing): When you think you are the only one in the marriage with skills, gifts, and talents, you really don't have a team. Normally, we say that TEAM stands for "Together Everyone Accomplishes More." While this is a true sentiment, it only works when the egos are nonexistent. When one spouse is prideful, the other will not be valued.

REVAMP (Review Exchanged Vows As Marital Promises): Are you a promise-keeper or a promise-breaker? On your wedding day, you made some promises to stick with your spouse. Did you mean them? You vowed to love and to cherish, for better or worse, for richer or poorer, in sickness and in health. If you meant those promises, keep them.

WAR (Words Affect Resolution): The words we use can help and heal or hurt and hinder. Proverbs 16:24 says, "Pleasant words are as a honeycomb, sweet to the soul, and health to the bones." Paul says, "Let no corrupt communication proceed out of your mouth, but that which is good to the use of edifying, that it may minister grace to the hearers" (Ephesians 4:29). You must be selective with your words. By the way, the old cliché is so far from the truth. "Sticks and stones may break my bones but names will never hurt me." Words *do* hurt. Proverbs 12:18 says, "Reckless words pierce like a sword."

SWAP (Speaking Without Addressing Problems): Talking a lot does not necessarily resolve conflict. As a matter of fact, you can talk too much. After you have finished talking for hours, the issue can still remain untouched. Why is this? We have talked more than we have listened. Proverbs 13:3 says, "He that keepeth his mouth keepeth his life: but he that openeth wide his lips shall have destruction."

Proverbs 18:13 says, "He that answers a matter before he heareth it, it is a folly and shame to him." I believe God had something special in mind when he created us with mouths that open and close and ears that remain open. I think He desires for us to listen more than talk.

KISS (Kindness Involves Speaking Softly): It is extremely difficult to have an intelligent conversation when people are yelling and screaming at the top of their lungs. The Bible says, "A soft answer turneth away wrath; but grievous words stir up anger" (Proverbs 15:1).

STEW (Scheduling Time Eliminates Wars): As mentioned before, you must take the time to communicate daily. Most of the conflict that surfaces in a relationship is the result of not spending enough time communicating.

MEAN (Mandatory Emotional Adjustment Needed): It is important to have an "attitude check" before trying to resolve an issue. Proverbs 14:29 says, "He that is slow to wrath is of great understanding:

but he that is hasty of spirit exalteth folly." If you think negatively, when you speak it will come out negatively. You need to take a time out to make an emotional adjustment.

ANGER (Asking Nicely Gets Effective Results): A tactful approach is needed to resolve conflict. Proverbs 17:27, 28a says, "He that hath knowledge spareth his words; and a man of understanding is of an excellent spirit. Even a fool, when he holdeth his peace, is counted wise." When issues surface, ask your spouse about them in the nicest way possible. Kindness begets kindness and yelling begets yelling.

TERMS (Truth Expressed Resolves Matters Swiftly): Issues cannot be resolved unless the truth is spoken. Proverbs 12:17 says, "He that speaketh truth sheweth forth righteousness; but a false witness deceit." Proverbs 13:5 says, "A righteous man hateth lying: but a wicked man is loathsome, and cometh to shame." Lying is always sinful and dangerous. There are always consequences to lying. Talk alone does not resolve conflict but *truthful* talking does. Proverbs 28:13 says, "He that covereth his sins shall not prosper: but whoso confesseth and forsaketh them shall have mercy."

DEPART (Don't Ever Publicly Address Relationship Turmoil): You should always seek to resolve conflict one-on-one or with a counselor and not at a family gathering, church seminar, or any other place where people are gathered. There is a time and place to deal with all issues. Proverbs 15:23 says, "A man hath joy by the answer of his mouth: and a word spoken in due season, how good is it!" It is good when it is spoken in "due season." Have you ever gone to a public function and witnessed a married couple arguing over their problems? This is not good.

FACE (Fatigue Affects Communication's Effectiveness): When you are exhausted, you sometimes say things that you don't mean or remember. Proverbs 3:24 says, "When thou liest down, thou shalt not be afraid: yea, thou shalt lie down, and thy sleep shall be sweet." The enemy knows that when we are mentally and physically exhausted, it is difficult to resolve a problem.

SMART (Sex Made After Resolving Trouble): When the winter is over, look forward to the springtime of intimacy. In one of Solomon's songs, he says, "My beloved spake, and said unto me, 'Rise up, my love, my fair one, and come away. For, lo, the winter is past, the rain is over and gone" (Song of Solomon 2:10-11). Making up after conflict has been resolved can offer the best lovemaking episodes that married couples will ever experience.

THE ROLES RIGHTLY UNDERSTOOD

Specific Scriptures address the roles in marriage. The roles aren't the problem per se. The problem is that people don't view the Bible as a sacred book that they are commanded to obey. For Christians, the Bible should serve as our manual for living. If you don't care what the Bible says about the matter, your marriage will never be what God desires.

The Caretaker's Responsibility

In Ephesians 5:23, Paul says, "For the husband is the head of the wife, even as Christ is the head of the church; and he is the savior of the body." Men have been given a special position in the marriage. The husband is to *serve* as the head of the wife and family.

Men, before you stick your chest out, let's make sure we know what this means. As a matter of fact, look at what Paul says a few verses later in the same chapter of Ephesians. He said, "Husbands, love your wives, even as Christ also loved the church, and gave himself for it" (Ephesians 5:25). Therefore, headship is not a position of power but a position of privilege.

Force and domination describe secular not spiritual leadership. As the head of the marriage, the husband is not the dictator; he is the servant or caretaker. The position is not about rank but responsibility; not about the title possessed but the tasks performed. This servant style of leadership focuses on "What can I give?" The dictator style of leadership focuses on "What can I gain?"

Let's examine a few areas (decisions, discussions, duties, desires, and deficiencies) and show the differences between the dictator style and the servant style.

How do the two styles look when the husband makes *Decisions* in the family?

- **Dictator style:** He gives orders and expects the orders to be obeyed. Others are not invited to offer their opinions. When a question or suggestion surfaces, it is viewed as an act of defiance.

- **Servant style:** He welcomes the opinions of others. He listens to suggestions that may differ from his. He is concerned about making the best decision. It doesn't matter who gets the credit.

    How do the two styles show up during *Discussions* in the family?

- **Dictator style:** Conversations are foreign. He often tries to prove his manhood by raising his voice or fist. He often intimidates his wife and she becomes afraid to discuss issues.

- **Servant style:** He enjoys having discussions with his wife. He will not raise his fist to show that he is the "man." He does not verbally abuse her.

    Let's look at the different approaches when it comes to the *Duties* in the home.

- **Dictator style:** He expects the wife to do it all. He feels that he can order the wife to take care of everything. She should feed him, take care of the kids, keep the house spotless, etc.

- **Servant style:** He tries to help out wherever and whenever needed. He doesn't view his wife as the "Superwoman."

    How do the two approaches look when it comes to *Desires* being fulfilled?

- **Dictator style:** He makes sure his desires are fulfilled. He ignores his wife's desires. Affection is something foreign to him.
- **Servant style:** He doesn't view his wife as a sex object but an object of affection. He desires to fulfill her desires. He takes the necessary steps for mutual satisfaction.

What about addressing *Deficiencies*?

- **Dictator style:** He points out faults, flaws, and failures. He can find fault in everything. Compliments are rarely offered.
- **Servant style:** He looks for the good to comment on. He addresses faults tactfully. He compliments her hair, food, attire, etc.

The Complementary Role

The wife is to submit to her own husband. Many women struggle with the term "submission" because it appears to point to a subservient state of existence. But from a biblical perspective, this is not the case at all. The term actually stems from the first description of the first wife in human history.

In the book of Genesis, Eve was described as the "helpmeet" for Adam. She was not created to be subservient to him, but to support him. Her role was not as a servant, but as a helper.

A perfect example of this can be seen in the cockpit of a 727 airplane. You have both the pilot and the co-pilot, who are equally qualified to fly the plane. Without assistance from the co-pilot, the plane would never fly as it was designed. The participation of both parties is required for the plane to take off, fly, and land safely. The same is true for the husband/wife team.

In Ephesians 5:22-24, Paul said, "Wives, submit yourselves unto your own husbands, as unto the Lord. For the husband is the head of the wife, even as Christ is the head of the church: and he is the savior of the body. Therefore as the church is subject unto Christ, so let the wives be to their own husbands in everything."

First, we have the *Expectation*. Submission is not something the husband created for his own satisfaction and gratification. The wife is commanded by God to submit, to obey, or to be in subjection to her husband. In other words, God expects it to happen. When you view your submission as rendering a service to the Lord, you are motivated to do it.

Next, we have the *Explanation*. In Ephesians 5:22, Paul says that the reason the wife is to be submissive is because "the husband is the head of the wife." God designed it this way. He did it for the purpose of having organization in the institution He established.

Look at the *Example* used in the passage. Paul gives the perfect example when he says, "as the church is subject to Christ" (Ephesians 5:24). The church must submit to the head, Jesus Christ.

Paul also addresses the *Extent* of the submission. Paul says that the wife is to submit "in everything." Submission is not to be an on-again, off-again matter or a selective process for the wife.

In Ephesians 5:25, he gives the *Encouragement* for the wife to submit. It is not difficult for a wife to be submissive when the husband is willing to love his wife as Christ loved the church. Submission is easier with a God-fearing husband. By the way, this unconditional love requires the husband to love his wife even during the unlovable moments.

In Colossians, Paul deals with the *Exception* to the command for the wife to submit. In Colossians 3:18, Paul says, "Wives, submit yourselves unto your own husbands, as it is fit in the Lord." Submission should occur as long as it is not sinful. If what is requested of you is not "fit unto the Lord," you are not to do it. Why? God holds each of us accountable for the sins we commit.

In Ephesians 5:18, Paul reveals the *Enabler* provided for the wife to be submissive and the husband to love his wife as Christ loved the church. With the help of the Holy Spirit, it can be done. The Holy Spirit serves as our Enabler.

If there is an unmarried man or woman thinking about marriage and reading this book, we want to re-emphasize the importance of making sure you are equally-yoked in your relationship. It takes a God-fearing man to love like Christ. It takes a God-fearing woman to submit as it is fit unto the Lord.

Chapter Nine

MAKING THE MARRIAGE ADULTERY-PROOF

The Cheating Refused

In Proverbs 5:18-20, we have some great advice to help guard against extramarital affairs. The writer says, "Let thy fountain be blessed: and rejoice with the wife of thy youth. Let her be as the loving hind and pleasant roe; let her breasts satisfy thee at all times: and be thou ravished always with her love. And why will thou, my son, be ravished with a strange woman, and embrace the bosom of a stranger?"

This passage contains several important points.

This proverb reveals the *Stupid Step* taken when intercourse occurs outside of marriage. Why embrace a stranger? The point is that you have no business connected with an outsider for sexual pleasure. Why not? It is due to the *Sexual Sin*. Any sex outside of marriage is sinful. Embracing the bosom of a stranger in deed or thought is stupid. Next, you need to be blessed by the *Supplied Spouse* God has given you in this area. Stick with the spouse supplied by the Savior.

Your spouse should be able to supply the *Sensual Satisfaction* you require. Stay sexually satisfied with your spouse "at all times." Learn your mate's love language and respond accordingly. Married couples need to beware of the seductive stranger out there. The *Seductive Stranger* is used to stir up the flesh (1 John 2:16). The seductive stranger is one of the *Satanic Schemes* designed to go against the institution established by God. The devil knows when to strike! He knows when there's turmoil and disunity in the home and he's betting on you to yield to his devices.

Let's address the *Special Size* of the seductive stranger. The satanic scheme matches your desire; that is, the shape, size, height, etc., of your lust. If you've thought of it, he has it! Just what your flesh desires at that moment is available. You need to also be aware of the *Simple Setup* whereby the seductive stranger shows up everywhere. Opportunities always surface to lead us down the wrong path. You don't have to be on a month-long work assignment out of town for the seductive stranger to surface. It can happen at the gym where you work out and at the church where you attend. Yield not to temptation!

The last comment for now deals with the *Sinful Stronghold*. If it happens once, it becomes easier to do it the second time. Before long, a stronghold is formed. Once you become addicted, it's extremely difficult to be released from it.

The Creeping Rejected

In Pastor Wesley's first marriage book entitled *If This Marriage Was Made in Heaven, Why Am I Going through Hell?*, there is a chapter that deals with the "Mean Monster." The mean monster is not some strange man or woman outside the marriage. The mean monster is really the strategic satanic substance called the "lust of the flesh" (see 1 John 2:16). But if needed, Satan will also use the strange outsider to stir up the monster within us.

Let's examine what we can do to control our flesh and prevent conflict in our marriages.

Run for Cover

We can't handle temptation on our own. Once you recognize this fact, you're on the right track. If you have to continuously repeat the statement, "I can handle this," you probably can't. Run, baby, run!

Regain the Control

Running away does not remove the desire to feed the flesh, but it's the first step. You have to regain control of your lust, your eyes, and your flesh by doing a few things listed below.

Remember the Covenant

On your wedding day, what did you promise? To whom did you commit? You promised to be faithful to your spouse alone. Don't forget the covenant.

Recite the Commandments

This is a good time to speak the Word! In the Ten Commandments, God said, "Thou shall not commit adultery." You should repeatedly speak this command until it sinks into your spirit. "Marriage is honourable in all, and the bed undefiled: but who remongers and adulterers God will judge" (Hebrews 13:4).

Renew the Commitment

When the flesh is stirred, renew your commitment to Christ. The thought of sinning is a sin. Jesus discussed this matter in the Sermon on the Mount. In Matthew 5:28, Jesus said, "But I say unto you, that whosoever looketh on a woman to lust after her hath committed adultery with her already in his heart." However, you have time to renew your commitment to Christ before making matters worse. David had a chance to renew his commitment after he saw Bathsheba bathing, but he chose not to do it. It is time to recommit to holiness, to obedience to the Word, and to your spouse.

Replace the Concentration

Instead of focusing on the tempting desire to sin, find something wholesome and holy to think about. Start reading your Bible, sing a gospel song, listen to music, or call a saved and sanctified believer.

Recognize the Come-On

The enemy seeks to attract and then attack. There's nothing wrong with receiving compliments from the other sex; but brothers, when a woman compliments you on your cologne by getting close to your body, sniffing your neck, and touching, that's a come-on! By the same token, ladies, when a man tells you how good you look in that dress and how it's hugging you in all "the right places" rather than simply saying "That's a nice dress," it's more than a compliment. Recognize!

Reject the Compliments

When you recognize the compliments as a come-on, you must reject them immediately. They're only stepping-stones to higher heights of temptation. If he tells you the dress is hugging you in all the right places, don't place your hands on your hips and model for him.

Retire the Collection

Get rid of your collection of contacts. Get rid of the little black, blue, or brown book of former "lovers" and such. Also, in our technological age, we need to erase the email addresses, number in our cell phones, cancel the "friend" status on Facebook, refuse to communicate through Twitter, etc.

Refuse the Company

Hang out with godly men and women. Notice we didn't say, "Hang out with church men and women," but godly people. It's sad to say, but there is a difference! Godly men and women walk in obedience to the Scriptures.

Reduce the Contacts

Take some extra steps to avoid contact with those who would tempt you. This may mean making sure that someone else is nearby when there's a meeting at the office or refusing to have meetings after hours. As a pastor, I never meet with a single woman alone. Not only that, but in my counseling sessions with females, my Administrative Assistant is always within earshot. That is by design.

Review the Consequences

Give some thought to what could happen if you engage in the sinful relationship. When you stop to think about what could happen to those you love if they found out, would you continue? What will be the repercussions to your spouse, children, family members, church members, and entire community of faith? More importantly, how would your relationship with God change? Think before you act!

Relish the Cleanliness

Sexual relationships outside of your marriage can literally destroy you and your spouse. We often told our sons when they were younger that you can't look at someone and ascertain if they have a sexually transmitted disease! Although STDs are treatable, most are not curable, and they come with all types of risks. Are you willing to take that chance?

Resolve the Conflict

Correct the division and discord at home. Whatever is out of order at home, resolve it! Life is short and opportunities pass quickly. Sit down and discuss what's needed to make the marriage work.

Repair the Communication

Keep the lines of communication open at all times.

Restore the Communion

Go to bed. After resolving conflict and repairing the lines of communication, do what married people are permitted to do. Make up and mess up the bed . . . and we don't mean to sleep!

Report the Contacts

Share the info with your accountability partner. The accountability partner is someone other than your spouse who is spiritually mature. When Satan tempts you, it is good to have an accountability partner to call so that you can be advised and encouraged to avoid the enemy's trap. Refuse to keep the encounter a secret, for that's where the enemy dwells.

Respect the Comments

Your spouse has valuable information about the seductive stranger. A woman knows a woman and man knows a man. If your spouse is a mature Christian, listen to what is being shared with you. Sometimes we can be naïve as it relates to the opposite sex, but our spouses can see what's going on. Listen and trust their instincts.

Refuse to Compromise

Avoid getting entangled in compromising positions. You know what these compromising positions are. They are the after-hour meetings, road trips, class reunions, etc. Make the necessary adjustments and don't get caught by the mean monster of temptation.

Run to the Commander in Chief

Jesus Christ is more powerful than the mean monster. When we yield to His directives, we'll be victorious! Scripture tells us that with every temptation, He has made a way for us to escape it (1 Corinthians 10:13). Take the escape route!

The Censored Routines

There is another area to address before leaving this subject matter. You may have a great track record in fighting off temptation. The strange men or women chasing after you have learned that you will not give them the time of day. You are to be commended for this record. However, there is another area to address.

Sin is not just based on what we do; it also includes our thoughts. Let me address some areas in which many married men and women are guilty.

The Pornographic Scene

The wicked worldwide web (wwww) has destroyed what God meant for good. It has helped to pervert the lives of many people. Christians should not visit pornographic sites in any form, including television and telephone programs.

The Personal Satisfaction

There should be mutual sexual satisfaction when making love. Your spouse is not a porn star! When you become infatuated and addicted to pornography, you begin to expect your spouse to perform those "circus acts" in the bedroom. Sex in marriage is designed to be pleasurable for both spouses, not just to satisfy the whims of one. Changing and experimenting with positions is fine as long as both are willing, no one is injured, and mutual satisfaction occurs.

The Private Sessions

The spouse God provided you with should never be replaced with private sessions. It is not the will of God for you to have private sessions of sexual pleasure (fingers, toys, pillows, etc.) when God has provided you with a spouse. It is permissible to tell your spouse what you like and where you like it.

The Powerful Savior

There is absolutely no bondage too hard for Him to break. If indeed one or both spouses have become addicted to pornography, self-gratification, or any sexual sin, remember that Jesus Christ is the bondage breaker. You can be victorious in this area of your life!

Chapter Ten

THE MESSAGE OF THE CROSS

~❦~

The Cross Remembered

Let's start off this section by reviewing the *Calvary Application*. It is necessary to go to the cross and remember what Christ did for all of us. Jesus paved the way for us to be forgiven of our sins when He died on the cross in our place. The cross should remind us that we have been forgiven. None of the material covered in this book will help couples if you are not willing to forgive each other. If you want the marriage to work as God intended, you must be willing to forgive.

What is the key to managing conflict? It is forgiveness. The *Continuous Act* of forgiving each other must take place. The key to living with another person in

an intimate relationship for many years is the ability
to forgive. Forgiveness is the oil of relationships. An
unforgiving partner in a marriage destroys the possibility
of a long-lasting and loving relationship.

In Ephesians 4, Paul was writing to a new group of
Christian believers who had come to Christ out of a
pagan culture. The norm was not forgiveness. The norm
was vengeance, retaliation, and anger. And now Paul is
going to teach them a new and better way – the way of
forgiveness. The heart of Ephesians 4:25-32 is the last
verse: "And be ye kind to one another, tenderhearted,
forgiving one another, even as God for Christ's sake
hath forgiven you."

An unforgiving spirit will lead to a *Contaminated
Atmosphere* in the marital relationship. Unresolved
conflict pollutes and contaminates the atmosphere of
forgiveness. The general atmosphere where forgiveness
can thrive is one not filled with what Paul mentions
in verse 31: "bitterness, and wrath, and anger, and
clamor, and evil speaking . . . with all malice." When
we allow disagreements and conflicts to go unchecked
and unresolved, they begin to pollute the atmosphere
in which we live. We must "put away from us" all those
practices so that an atmosphere conducive to forgiveness
can be created.

The *Correct Attitude* regarding forgiveness must exist in order for the relationship to remain intact. Forgiveness must be done with tenderness. The attitude necessary for forgiveness can be summarized in one word: "tenderhearted" (v. 32). Have you ever heard someone say, "All right, I forgive you if that's what you want"? This is not a tenderhearted approach to the conflict. When there is an edge in our voice, tenderheartedness disappears and the words lose their power to reconcile.

Forgiveness often means tears and almost always means gentle, soft words of humility. The asking for and extending of forgiveness is not a loud, boisterous event. The only reason the need for forgiveness exists is because someone has been hurt or offended. And the realization that you have hurt the person you love brings sorrow and humility. That's tenderheartedness.

Let me comment on the *Culture's Approach* as it relates to men here. Men, in my experience, need to devote more attention to tenderheartedness than their wives. Our culture does not reward the idea of tenderness in men, so we tend to keep up the outward façade of strength, refusing to participate in the tenderness that forgiveness requires. You will still be known as a strong man in society when you display tenderheartedness in your relationships.

The Charges Removed

In Ephesians 4:25-27, 32, Paul describes the steps required to remove the charges against the ones who have offended us.

Let's look at the *Specific Acknowledgment* required when it comes to forgiving one another. Verse 25 says to speak truth with our neighbor, that is, to one another. Truth means honesty and frankness. Forgiveness cannot take place unless the specific act (commission or omission) is acknowledged and confessed. Otherwise, there is nothing to forgive. Here is a truthful and frank approach: "Honey, I am truly sorry for what I said earlier tonight. It was thoughtless and insensitive on my part. I know that I hurt you by my words, and I understand why you are hurt. And I want to ask you to forgive me for what I said."

Have you heard this one before? "I am sorry for any hurt my words and actions may have caused." Wrong! This places the burden on the person who was hurt. The speaker does not think his words or actions were wrong; he is only acknowledging that someone was weak enough to be hurt by the words or actions. There is no personal confession or honest acknowledgment that what the person said or did was wrong.

It is also wrong for the hurt person to minimize the pain he or she is experiencing: "It's okay; don't worry about it." Wrong! It wasn't okay. It hurt you and you must be frank about it. Forgiveness requires frankness (honesty) by both spouses in order for conflicts to be resolved.

Next, let's look at the need for *Swift Action* to fix the matter at hand. In verses 26-27, Paul says not to let the sun go down on our anger. That applies to any relationship, of course, but especially in marriage where you are spending the night with the person toward whom you have anger, or who is angry at you. Paul is saying to make sure all the conflicts you face are today's conflicts, not yesterday's. When an offense is recognized, and forgiveness is necessary, deal with it as promptly as you can. The longer you wait, the more difficult it is to come back to it and get it straight.

If we don't deal with things as promptly as possible, the issues do not go away. They get buried alive in the very heart of our being. And when that happens, the offense finds fertile soil in which a root of bitterness can sink deep and begin to bear fruit (Hebrews 12:15). Huge explosions of anger by a spouse in marriage are nothing more than the accumulated pressure of offenses swept under the rug. They will eventually find their way to the surface and require even additional forgiveness. Before long, all arguments become based on past wrongs committed and the present issues remained unresolved.

We must guard against the *Sought Amendment* to the offense committed. In Ephesians 4:32 Paul says, ". . . forgiving one another." There is no condition to forgiveness. It is not "forgive if. . . ." It is just "forgive." Too often in marriage we speak in terms of conditions: "I will apologize for what I did if you apologize for what you did." Or "I will forgive you if you forgive me."

The *Standard Applied* for how much we are to forgive, or to what extent, is found in verse 32. We are to forgive fully, the same way God forgives us. God doesn't forgive most of our sin or our sin up to failure number 100 and nothing after that. No, He forgives all of our sin: past, present, and future. The blood of Jesus does not simply address our BC (Before Christ) sins. All of our sins were covered by His death on Calvary. The couple serious about forgiving as God forgives will view all their spouse's sins in the future as already forgiven.

True forgiveness happens when *Selective Amnesia* is used. Forgiveness is to be once and for all. In Isaiah 43:25 God says, "I, even I, am he that blotteth out thy transgressions for mine own sake, and will not remember thy sins." When people say, "I can forgive, but I can't forget," I tell them, "Fine. Just decide not to remember." You cannot erase what happened in the past, but you can choose not to keep it current and replay the tapes daily. If it is forgiven, it's final.

The Christian Requirement

Forgiveness is the *Mandatory Step* required of all Christians. We have been commanded by God to forgive one another. Whatever God has commanded us to do, He equips us to do. Since God requires us to forgive, it is something we can do. But forgiveness is difficult for us. Why? Forgiveness pulls against our concept of justice. We want revenge for offenses suffered. But we are told never to take our own revenge (see Romans 12:19). You say, "Why should I let him/her off the hook?" That's precisely the problem. You are "still hooked" to them, still bound by your past. The objective is to take them off of your hook and place them on God's hook. Why does God require us to forgive?

He requires it because of the *Manipulative Scheme* of the enemy. We need to forgive others so that Satan cannot take advantage of us. In 2 Corinthians 2:10-11, Paul says, "To whom ye forgive anything, I forgive also: for if I forgave anything, to whom I forgave it, for your sakes forgave I it in the person of Christ. Lest Satan should get an advantage of us: for we are not ignorant of his devices." Satan knows I cannot get better when I am bitter.

Since it is a requirement as it relates to marriage, you are to be the *Merciful Spouse*. We are to be merciful just as our heavenly Father is merciful. Jesus says, "Be ye therefore merciful, as your Father also is merciful" (Luke 6:36). As mentioned before, mercy involves not giving the person what he/she rightly deserves based on his or her actions (sin).

We have the *Motivating Source* to help us meet this requirement. We are to forgive as we have been forgiven. In Ephesians 4:32, Paul says, "And be ye kind one to another, tenderhearted, forgiving one another, *even as God for Christ's sake hath forgiven you.*" In the verse preceding this command, we are told to put away bitterness, wrath, anger, clamor, and evil speaking. Aren't you glad God does not hold grudges? Neither should we. When you review your own story of being forgiven by God, it should motivate you to forgive others.

Forgiveness is often viewed the wrong way. Let's deal with the *Misinterpreted Step* often linked to forgiveness. I am sure you have heard someone say, "I cannot forgive and forget." Forgiveness is not forgetting. People who try to forget find they cannot. God says He will remember our sins "no more" (see Hebrews 10:17), but God, being omniscient, cannot forget. Remember our sins "no more" means that God will never use the past against us (Psalm 103:12). Forgetting may be the result of forgiveness, but it is never the means of forgiveness. When we bring up the past against others, we are saying we haven't forgiven them.

Have you given any thought to the *Miraculous Substitution* that occurred in order for us to be redeemed? All true forgiveness is substitutionary. God the Father "made Him who knew no sin to be sin on our behalf, so that we might become the righteousness of God in Him" (2 Cor. 5:21 NASB). Jesus served as the substitute for our sins. When we forgive, we are agreeing to live with the consequences of another person's sin. Forgiveness is costly. You pay the price for the evil you forgive. However, you're going to live with those consequences whether you want to or not. It just seems better to live with the consequences without carrying the load of bitterness around.

If you are ready to forgive, it is time to truly take a trip to the *Mercy Seat* of God. In the Old Testament, the high priest took the blood from a sacrificed lamb into the Holy of Holies and sprinkled it on the mercy seat, God's throne to make atonement for the sins committed by the people during the year. As Christians, we have direct access to the throne through Jesus Christ. First, you must take the offenses committed against you by your spouse and others to the mercy seat. In order for this to happen, you must be real about your pain. Next, you must acknowledge the hurt and hate you feel as a result of what your spouse did. This is where the healing begins to take place. You cannot be healed without making this acknowledgment first.

Now you must decide to forgive the offender for the offense committed. Don't wait to forgive until you feel like forgiving; you will never get there. Neither should you wait for the offender to ask for forgiveness; this may never happen. Lastly, you must decide that you will not use the information against your spouse in the future. This does not mean that you must tolerate sin; you must always take a stand against sin.

Remember that forgiveness is dealing with your pain and leaving the offender to God. Therefore, it is totally out of order for you to go to your spouse with the finger pointed or the hand on the hip, saying, "I want you to know I forgave you today when I prayed." This becomes a tool for the enemy to use to try and stir up strife again.

Before concluding this chapter, we would like to share an exercise we use in the marriage seminars we conduct. We have a huge cross on the stage with several paper shredders in front of it. We separate the husbands and wives to opposite sides of the room. We give each of them a sheet of paper with the information listed and on the following page, they are directed to write down the spouse's name, and to list the offenses that they have not really forgiven them for, then they are to pray the brief prayer for each one.

Lord, I forgive _____ (spouse's name) for (specifically identify all offenses and painful memories or feelings):

1.

2.

3.

4.

5.

6.

7.

After completing these steps, we have to take the list to the cross. Place the completed list in the shredder. After this is done, you are *free*!

Chapter Eleven

MARRIAGE MAINTENANCE TIPS

We would like to conclude this book by sharing a few marriage maintenance tips that may prove to be helpful. As we prepare to end our time with you, let's consider a few more steps (*quickies*) to take in order to improve your marriage.

There is a need for *Continuous Renewal* in our marriages. It takes more than attending a seminar or reading a marriage book to keep our marriages thriving. It would be wonderful to attend a marriage enrichment seminar for a few weeks and end up correcting all marriage woes. It doesn't work this way. Continuing steps must be taken to make the marriage better. There is not a "quick fix." Yet there will be visible improvements when both parties commit to work on the marriage.

Next, in our marriages we need to implement a *Cautious Reaction* to what is not factual. Stop jumping to conclusions. As noted before, we need to be "slow to speak." There are times when issues surface and we react to what we perceive rather than waiting to hear from God and our spouse concerning the matter.

Men, this one is specifically for us. It deals with the *Calendar Remembered*. Don't forget the important days (birthdays, anniversaries, etc.). You cannot maintain a healthy marriage by simply remembering the holiday on the calendar. The candy, champagne, and candlelight on special days are extremely important.

When you choose to work on your marriage instead of end it, the *Criticism Received* from others may surprise you. We know of spouses who have forgiven their mates for being unfaithful. By doing this, they had another matter to deal with. There were outsiders aware of the infidelity and added their "two cents." When you choose to forgive your spouse for being unfaithful, the critics will surface. They will say, "You must be crazy going back to her." "You took him back but he's going to do it again." Don't listen to them. Keep loving your spouse and trusting in God.

Continuous Rejection of your spouse's sexual advances can be destructive. Married people are permitted to make love. Marriage is honorable and the bed is undefiled. It is your God-given duty to engage in sexual activity when your spouse desires to (see 1 Cor. 7:3-5). We must be careful when we deny him or her sexually. We are going against the Word of God when we do so. If a cold reception is continuously given to your spouse, it can easily become the norm without your realizing it. Rejection always stirs up the flesh and gives the devil ammunition to use against the marriage.

Do what is necessary to keep the *Courtship Rekindled*. Keep courting your spouse! On a regular basis, renew the days of courtship. Go ahead and do some of the things you enjoyed doing together before the kids and career came along.

Next, you need to take intentional steps to keep the *Chemistry Revived* in your marriage. There was a time when you could not keep your hands off of each other in an intimate fashion. What happened to those days? If the chemistry once existed, it is just a matter of relocating and reviving it. When you are trying to find something, it is important to think back to the time when you had it last. You can also have a situation where it is in a place nearby and you are looking in the wrong places.

Let's deal with *Courteous Routines* in the marriage. Common courtesy can prevent unnecessary conflict. A lot of couples would have a better relationship if they used simple common courtesy. For example, if you are going to be late coming home from the office, let your spouse know. A simple call can prevent worry.

Beware of the *Coming Robber*. The devil will not withdraw his forces because you attended a marriage seminar or read this book about marriage. You can implement every step outlined in this material and think your marriage issues will be resolved. In the Scripture, the enemy is described as a thief who comes to rob, steal, and destroy. The devil will continue to attack. However, he knows he's in trouble because he is dealing with a stronger spiritual couple now.

The good news is that you have the *Comforter Residing* in your life and the enemy cannot handle Him. You are not alone in this fight for your marriage. God can handle whatever the devil tries to do. Whatever God commands us to do, He also equips us to get it done. He will help you to do what you cannot do on your own.

It is your responsibility to keep the *Companionship Recognized* even when your spouse is not present. Do things to show the fact that you are married. People in the public arena should know you are a married man or woman.

Since we have the *Competing Realities* of life on our shoulders, it is important to keep the *Covenant's Rules* prioritized over everything else. The covenant must be prioritized over all other competing realities like children and careers. If you don't keep things in their proper perspective, your marriage will suffer. I have always tried to focus on being a partner to my spouse, a parent to my boys, and a pastor to the flock. This is the correct order.

Men, this is another one for us. It deals with the *Compliments Rendered* to our spouses. Compliment your spouse regularly. Once again, if you don't, the enemy will set it up so that someone will.

Let's deal with the *Complaining Regiment* in some marriages. There is no place for constant complaining in our marriages. Compliments paid will not be effective if complaints outweigh them. You must work on reducing complaints. You may be concerned that I am saying reduce the complaints rather than stop the complaining. Let's keep it real. In our marriages, there are things we don't like and we must address them. It is the way we do it that will help the marriage flow as God intended.

Be mindful of the *Checkups Required* to keep the marriage thriving. Don't stop tuning up your marriage by simply reading a book or two on marriage. We have our cars serviced continuously to make sure that they will last as long as possible. If you fail to change the oil on a regular basis, you can mess up the engine. Take the time to attend married couples classes, marriage enrichment seminars, or retreats just to make sure you are still on the right road.

The last comment in this book is probably the most important point of them all. The *Contacted Redeemer* is the key to a successful marriage. Spend quality time in your secret closet praying without ceasing. Not only should you pray for your spouse and the marriage, you should also pray for God to show you ways to improve as far as your involvement is concerned.

CPSIA information can be obtained
at www.ICGtesting.com
Printed in the USA
FSOW02n1551020715
8499FS

CONTACT INFORMATION

REDEMPTION
PRESS

To order additional copies of this book, please visit
www.redemption-press.com.
Also available on Amazon.com and BarnesandNoble.com
Or by calling toll free 1-844-2REDEEM.